Original title:
Winds of the Wildlands

Copyright © 2024 Creative Arts Management OÜ
All rights reserved.

Author: Riley Hawthorne
ISBN HARDBACK: 978-9916-88-868-1
ISBN PAPERBACK: 978-9916-88-869-8

The Solace of Untamed Horizons

Beneath the wide and open sky,
Waves of grass in breezes sigh.
Mountains stand with noble grace,
Time stands still in nature's embrace.

Golden fields where shadows play,
Chasing clouds that drift away.
Each horizon calls the heart,
A canvas where new dreams can start.

Landscapes of Whispered Dreams

In valleys deep, soft echoes call,
Where whispers rise and shadows fall.
Moonlit nights paint stories bright,
Guiding souls through gentle light.

Ancient trees with secrets hold,
Roots entwined in tales of old.
Through winding paths, our spirits roam,
In this land, we find our home.

The Spirit of Roaming Guardians

With watchful eyes upon the land,
Guardians weave with gentle hands.
In the rustle of leaves, they dwell,
Their stories hidden, yet they tell.

From mountain peaks to rivers wide,
Their essence flows, a timeless guide.
In every creature and each tree,
A spirit roams, wild and free.

In Search of Earthbound Whispers

Through the meadows, soft and low,
Whispers wander, ebb and flow.
Seeking truth in shadows cast,
Moments cherished, memories past.

With every breeze, a secret shared,
In silent woods, the heart laid bare.
In earthbound whispers, souls unite,
In harmony beneath the night.

Beyond the Whispering Trees

In shadows deep where secrets lie,
Leaves rustle softly, a gentle sigh.
The wind carries tales of old,
Whispers of wonders yet to be told.

Moonlight dances on the brook,
Curious eyes in every nook.
The heart of nature pulses slow,
Beyond the whispering trees, we grow.

Horizon's Edge in Twilight's Glow

The sun dips low, the sky ablaze,
Painting the world in fiery haze.
Stars begin their joyous rise,
As twilight spreads across the skies.

Soft breezes carry the night's embrace,
Melodies hum in a gentle space.
At horizon's edge, dreams take flight,
In the whispers of the coming night.

Secrets in the Breath of the Forest

Amidst the trees, a silence deep,
Ancient secrets the branches keep.
Every rustle, a tale to spin,
In the forest's heart, life begins.

Moonbeams cascade through the leaves,
Telling stories that the night weaves.
In every shadow, a promise lies,
Secrets held where the wild heart sighs.

Songs of the Boundless Expanse

Across the fields where wild winds blow,
Nature sings in a vibrant flow.
Each note of grass, each song of sky,
Calls to the wanderer passing by.

Mountains echo with timeless grace,
Whispering dreams of a vast embrace.
In the boundless expanse, we are free,
In the songs of earth, our souls agree.

Shifting Shadows in Nature's Embrace

In the forest's heart, shadows play,
Dancing leaves in the waning day.
Whispers of breezes, soft and low,
Nature's secrets begin to flow.

Beneath the boughs, a silent call,
Creatures stir in the twilight's thrall.
Moonlight filters through tangled vines,
Painting the world in silver lines.

Echoes of life in the twilight hour,
A fusion of calm and nature's power.
With every rustle, a story told,
Of ancient paths and wonders bold.

In this embrace, we find our peace,
As shifting shadows grant release.
Moments captured in the evening's grace,
Forever cherished in nature's space.

Tales from the Wild Edges

Along the cliffs where wild winds blow,
The stories of nature start to flow.
Each crevice hides a whispered tale,
Of storms that came and fierce gales pale.

Beneath the stars, the night unfolds,
A canvas rich with legends old.
Creatures wander, and echoes thrill,
In untamed realms, where hearts are still.

The jagged rocks, they stand in pride,
Guarding secrets that the tides confide.
With every wave, a chapter turns,
In wild edges where freedom yearns.

Nature's pulse beats strong and grand,
In rugged landscapes, souls will stand.
With every breath, the wild calls free,
Tales from edges, forever to be.

Embrace of the Restless Gales

The restless gales weave through the trees,
Singing songs that embrace the seas.
Whispers of change in the swaying boughs,
Nature's dance in the moonlit vows.

As shadows stretch and merge with night,
The winds carry tales on wings of flight.
Every gust a brush of fate,
In the embrace where hearts await.

Through valleys deep and mountains high,
The gales rush forth, like fervent sighs.
With each caress, a promise made,
As the wild spirits begin to fade.

In every chorus, an echo stirs,
The heart remembers what nature stirs.
Beneath the stars, the gales sing strong,
In timeless rhythms where we belong.

The Song of Lost Valleys

In valleys deep where silence flows,
Nature's song in the twilight glows.
Echoes of dreams in the shadows lie,
Beneath the watchful, endless sky.

Memories of paths that once were clear,
Held in the whispers that we hold dear.
Forgotten tales carried by the breeze,
In hidden nooks among the trees.

The softest sighs of a fading light,
Bring echoes of day into the night.
Each lost valley a story spun,
Of battles fought and victories won.

Yet in the stillness, hope remains,
A quiet strength in nature's veins.
The song of lost valleys, forever shared,
In every heart where love has dared.

Shadows that Dance in Silence

In quiet corners where whispers dwell,
Shadows waltz under a faded spell.
Moonlight's gaze on the floor so bare,
Dances weave through the cool night air.

Echoes linger in the dim-lit room,
Softly draping the heart with gloom.
Each step traces tales of the past,
In the silence, their spell is cast.

Footsteps fade as the night grows old,
Secrets dance in hues of gold.
A fleeting glance, a lover's sigh,
In this silence, their hopes can fly.

With every breath, the shadows sway,
Guiding souls who have lost their way.
In the stillness, they find their chance,
To embrace the lost, in a shadowed dance.

Twilight Tales from the Edge of Tomorrow

At the brink of dusk, stories unfold,
Mysteries whisper, both timid and bold.
The horizon blushes in shades of gray,
As twilight beckons the stars to play.

A dreamer's heart beats fierce and fast,
With visions cast from shadows past.
Each twilight tale, a thread so fine,
Woven in time, like stars that shine.

Voices echo through the cooling night,
Crafting futures stitched in light.
From edges of dreams, the stories flow,
In the twilight's arms, where wishes grow.

Hope takes flight on the wings of dusk,
In silken dreams, we place our trust.
Beyond the veil where the night takes reign,
Twilight whispers of joys and pain.

Beneath the Canopy of Stars

Underneath the vast, ink-black skies,
A tapestry of dreams begins to rise.
Stars like lanterns scattered around,
Each twinkle tells a tale profound.

A gentle breeze kisses the night air,
Every leaf dances without a care.
In the quiet, stories softly hum,
Beneath the stars, we all come from.

The universe cradles our fears and hopes,
In cosmic rhythms, our spirit copes.
Guided by the shimmer of distant light,
We gather hearts beneath the night.

With each heartbeat, the cosmos sings,
Notes of wonder on shimmering wings.
Together, we dream beneath the sky,
Beneath the stars, we learn to fly.

Traces of Forgotten Footsteps

In the quiet woods, they fade,
Echoes of paths once made.
Whispers of travelers long gone,
Left in the light of the dawn.

Leaves crunch softly underfoot,
Memories where old dreams shoot.
Time weaves through each silent stream,
A tapestry of lost dream.

Faded signs on a mossy bark,
Each marking tells a hidden spark.
Nature holds secrets within,
Stories of where we've been.

Footprints in the dust of years,
Tell tales of joys and fears.
In shadows deep, they softly sleep,
Traces of past we wish to keep.

Between Sky and Wilderness

Where the horizon kisses the night,
Stars awaken with gentle light.
Clouds drift softly, whispers low,
In the heart of nature's flow.

Mountains rise, grace defined,
In their shadows, peace we find.
The breeze carries tales untold,
Of ancient stories, brave and bold.

Meadows dance in twilight's glow,
Secrets of the wild, they show.
With each step, spirits guide,
In the beauty of the untamed wide.

Together in this sacred place,
We seek the universe's embrace.
Between the sky and earth so vast,
A harmony that holds us fast.

In the Midst of Wildflowers

Colors burst in a vibrant sway,
Nature's quilt in bright array.
Petals whisper secrets soft,
In the air, dreams lift aloft.

Bees hum low, a sweet refrain,
In gardens where joy washes pain.
Each bloom tells a tale anew,
Of sunlit days and skies so blue.

Dancing lightly in the breeze,
Filling hearts with promises.
Their fragrance lingers, pure delight,
A canvas painted in soft light.

Among wildflowers, we find grace,
In every color, every place.
In their midst, we breathe and sigh,
With the wild we learn to fly.

Shadows of the Ancient Pines

In the grove where giants stand,
Roots embrace the timeless land.
Needles whisper in the air,
Secrets kept with tender care.

Moonlight filters through the leaves,
Casting magic that deceives.
In the stillness, spirits play,
Ancient wisdom holds sway.

Beneath the boughs, the world feels small,
Echoes of nature's primal call.
With every shadow, stories rise,
Of battles fought 'neath endless skies.

In their shade, we come alive,
With every breath, together thrive.
Among the ancient pines so tall,
We find the strength to stand, not fall.

Between Earth and Ether

In twilight's grace, the whispers play,
A dance of shadows, dusk turns to gray.
The stars awaken, twinkling bright,
As dreams take flight in the soft night.

With every breath, the silence sighs,
A secret world where magic lies.
Between the realms of here and there,
An echo calls through fragrant air.

Upon the hills, where shadows blend,
The heart finds peace, the soul can mend.
Through twilight's veil, we seek to roam,
In this embrace, we are at home.

So linger softly, time stands still,
In every heartbeat, in every thrill.
Between earth and ether, we reside,
In nature's arms, forever tied.

Where River Meets the Sky

Beneath the arch where waters flow,
And skies reflect their gentle glow.
The river sings a timeless song,
Where heartbeats mingle, right or wrong.

In whispered currents, stories blend,
Of lovers lost and wishes penned.
The sky unfolds in shades of blue,
As ripples dance, both bold and true.

The horizon stretches, dreams take wing,
In this embrace, the heart will sing.
Where land and heavens softly kiss,
A moment frozen, pure bliss.

Through every tide, the seasons shift,
In nature's bond, we find our gift.
Where river meets the endless sky,
In this sweet union, we learn to fly.

Echoes in the Wilderness

Among the trees where shadows play,
The wildwood speaks in a timeless way.
With every breath, the whispers grow,
In the quiet heart, the secrets flow.

Beneath the boughs, a story calls,
Of ancient lands and crumbling walls.
Echoes linger in the rustling leaves,
Where every heartache quietly grieves.

Footfalls tread on the mossy ground,
In this solitude, solace is found.
The streams murmur while stars align,
In the wilderness, our souls entwine.

With nature's grace, the world stands still,
In every heartbeat, we find our will.
Lost in echoes, we roam this space,
In the wild's embrace, we find our place.

Lullabies of Forgotten Trails

In moonlit glow, the pathways yearn,
Where whispers weave and lanterns burn.
The night hums soft, a gentle tune,
Beneath the watchful eyes of the moon.

Each step we take, a tale unfolds,
Of ancient woods and secrets bold.
The air is thick with dreams untold,
In every shadow, stories unfold.

Through twisted roots and craggy stones,
We seek to find the distant homes.
In lullabies, the wind doth sing,
Awakening hope in the soft spring.

With every journey, paths may fade,
Yet in our hearts, the memories stay.
Lullabies of trails long gone,
In twilight's glow, we carry on.

The Hush of Unseen Paths

In the quiet woods, secrets blend,
Whispers of ages that never end.
Footsteps light on mossy ground,
Echoes of journeys lost, yet found.

Beneath the boughs, shadows play,
Guiding the lost, showing the way.
Soft rustle in the gentle breeze,
Tales of wanderers, lost with ease.

Misty mornings hold their breath,
Moments alive, far from death.
Through tangled roots, dreams are spun,
The hush reveals where time has run.

Yet every turn, a choice to take,
Paths unfold, with each step we make.
In silence, wisdom's softly crowned,
In unseen paths, our fate is bound.

Soliloquy of the Moonlit Plains

Beneath the sky, the silver glows,
Moonlit whispers where the wild wind blows.
Fields stretch wide, a tranquil sea,
Nature's heart beats here, wild and free.

Stars above in a velvet shroud,
Glisten softly, speak aloud.
Nightingale sings a haunting tune,
Echoing dreams in the light of the moon.

Each blade of grass, a story weaved,
Of hopes and secrets that never grieved.
In the still, a gentle thrill,
Words of the night, a serene will.

The plains, they hush, as if to hear,
All that we love, all that is dear.
In the depths of night, we find our reign,
A soliloquy sung in moonlit plains.

The Pulse of the Untamed Land

Mountains rise, fierce and bold,
Guardians of tales, waiting to be told.
Rivers rush with ancient power,
Nature's heart beats hour by hour.

Through thickets deep, the wild resides,
In every rustle, adventure hides.
Echoes of creatures, proud and grand,
Mark the rhythm of untamed land.

The wind carries whispers of strife,
Every gust a pulse of life.
Between the trees, secrets flow,
The wildness within, begins to grow.

Here, the spirit roams so free,
In every heart, the wild will be.
Nature's pulse in every strand,
A song of freedom, untamed land.

Stories Carried by the Clouds

Clouds drift by in gentle grace,
Carrying tales from place to place.
Whispers of storms, of sunlit days,
Fragments of life in their soft haze.

Each shape a memory, lost but near,
A canvas of dreams, both far and dear.
Misty figures dance through the skies,
Painting the world with silent sighs.

In the twilight, they softly glow,
Tales of the earth in their ebb and flow.
Skyward travelers, in silence soar,
Bringing us stories, forevermore.

From the heights, hope showers down,
In every raindrop, a jewel crown.
In fleeting moments, wisdom found,
The stories whispered by the clouds abound.

Voice of the Verdant Earth

Whispers of leaves dance in the breeze,
Ancient roots speak in silent pleas.
Beneath the sky, where wildflowers sway,
Nature's chorus sings, day by day.

Mountains stand tall, draped in green,
Echoes of life in every scene.
Rivers flow, carrying tales anew,
The earth binds us, me and you.

In twilight's glow, shadows weave,
Crickets chirp, as the night takes leave.
A symphony of crickets and stars,
The world awakens, free from bars.

In harmony's grace, we all belong,
Together we rise, a united song.
Embrace the earth, feel her worth,
Listen closely to her gentle mirth.

The Spirit of Every Step

Every footfall is a message sent,
In each stride, a dream is lent.
Pavement whispers secrets untold,
The journey of life, a tale unfolds.

Sand beneath toes, a warm embrace,
The ocean's breath, a tranquil space.
Across the meadows, past the streams,
Each path traveled fuels new dreams.

In shadows cast by ancient trees,
Feel the spirit in the breeze.
With every step, a heartbeat found,
The world awakens, all around.

Let us wander where the wild winds lead,
In every journey, plant a seed.
In the rhythm of life, bound by fate,
The spirit of steps, truly great.

Memories of the Silent Beasts

In the forest, echoes of the past,
Silent creatures, shadows cast.
Faint footprints mark the forest floor,
Whispers of life, forevermore.

The owl's gaze, wise and deep,
Secrets locked, they silently keep.
Beneath the stars, the wild things roam,
In midnight stillness, they call it home.

Tales of the night, wrapped in mist,
Legacy of beasts that hardly exist.
With every heartbeat, nature sighs,
The dance of life, where magic lies.

Memories linger, softly fade,
In every shadow, a promise laid.
Nature's tapestry, rich and vast,
The silent beasts whisper of the past.

Rapture of the Roaming Clouds

Above the world, the clouds do play,
In shades of white, they drift and sway.
Caressed by light, they dance on high,
A sailing ship in the vast blue sky.

Whispers of rain begin to fall,
A gentle touch, a soft enthrall.
In twilight hues, they blush and gleam,
Heavenly bodies in a waking dream.

As day surrenders to the night,
Stars peek through, a dazzling sight.
Clouds transformed into shadows deep,
Guarding secrets the cosmos keep.

In their rapture, time stands still,
A canvas painted by nature's will.
Let your spirit soar, set it free,
In the roaming clouds, find your glee.

Murmurs Through the Ancient Woods

Whispers weave through branches tall,
Ancient tales that softly call.
Leaves rustle with secrets old,
In the woods, the magic unfolds.

Footsteps echo on the ground,
Nature's symphony surrounds.
Mossy carpets, soft and deep,
In this haven, dreams all sleep.

Sunlight dances, shadows play,
Time stands still in this ballet.
Every sound a timeless thread,
In the woods, the spirit's fed.

Murmurs of the past reside,
In the heart, where echoes glide.
Nature's voice will always stay,
Guiding souls who lose their way.

Call of the Free Spirit

Windswept shores and endless skies,
The free spirit yearns and flies.
With every wave, a new embrace,
In wild places, finds its grace.

Mountains rise with strength and pride,
In their shadows, dreams abide.
Chasing sunsets, racing dawn,
In the heart, the spirit's drawn.

Boundless roads and trails untold,
In their depths, adventures bold.
Every heartbeat sings a tune,
In the light of the silvery moon.

With open arms, the world awaits,
Embracing paths that destiny creates.
A call to wander, roam, and fly,
For the free spirit, the limit is the sky.

Shadows Under the Wide Sky

Beneath the vast and starlit night,
Shadows dance in soft moonlight.
Whispers linger as dreams take flight,
In the silence, hearts ignite.

Clouds drift slowly, casting doubt,
In this stillness, love's about.
Every star a tale to tell,
In the dark, where secrets dwell.

Gentle winds brush through the trees,
Carrying whispers of the breeze.
Underneath the wide expanse,
Life unfolds with every chance.

Lost in thoughts, I wander deep,
In the shadows, thoughts to keep.
Here beneath the vast night's sigh,
Awakened dreams begin to fly.

Tales Carried on the Gales

Listen close to the winds that speak,
Stories told, both strong and meek.
Through the valleys, hills, and dales,
Echo softly, tales on gales.

Mountains echo laughter and tears,
Every whisper carries years.
In the rustle of the leaves,
Ancient wisdom softly weaves.

With every breeze, a new refrain,
Linking past and future's chain.
Nature's breath, a storyteller,
In its arms, we all can dwell.

Hearts united, far and near,
In the stories, we hold dear.
Tales of love and dreams unfold,
On gales of time, forever told.

Murmurs of the Ancient Grove

Whispers weave through ancient trees,
As shadows dance upon the leaves.
Mossy roots in twilight's glow,
Secrets held that only they know.

A breeze carries tales of old,
In tangled limbs, their stories told.
The moon peeks through the verdant veil,
Guiding wanderers on the trail.

Each rustle speaks of days gone by,
Beneath the watchful starlit sky.
Echoes of history in each sigh,
Where time drifts slow and dreams can fly.

The grove enchants with its charm,
A sanctuary, safe and warm.
In its embrace, the mind can roam,
Finding peace, a primal home.

Horizon's Breath at Dusk

Golden hues kiss the fading light,
As day surrenders to the night.
Whispers of wind and waves entwined,
In twilight's glow, hope is defined.

The horizon stretches, wide and free,
A canvas painted endlessly.
Stars awaken, a gentle sigh,
As shadows gather, dreams comply.

Cool breezes carry secrets far,
While dusk unveils the evening star.
Ocean's lullaby, soft and sweet,
Where land and sky in stillness meet.

In the calm, heartbeats align,
With the pulse of earth and time.
Beneath this vast, embracing dome,
We find our way, our truest home.

Flickers of Light through the Canopy

Sunbeams pierce the leafy shield,
Painting patterns on the field.
Dappled moments, fleeting grace,
Nature's magic, a warm embrace.

Birdsongs echo through the air,
In the stillness, life feels rare.
Fingers of light reach out and play,
Guiding spirits along the way.

Gentle rustles mark the path,
Where each step ignites a laugh.
In this realm of emerald dreams,
The heart awakens, or so it seems.

Together we wander, lost yet found,
In the symphony of nature's sound.
For in this dance of shadow and gleam,
We weave our stories, thread by dream.

The Journey Beyond Familiar Shores

Waves crash upon the winding coast,
Carrying dreams, both fears and hopes.
With each tide, a call to roam,
To chase the stars and find a home.

Sailboats glide on horizons grand,
Charting courses across the sand.
Each anomaly, a tale untold,
In whispered winds, the brave are bold.

Beyond the reef, where oceans blend,
Lies adventure waiting 'round the bend.
Each heartbeat echoes with the sea,
The journey beckons, wild and free.

As far as dreams can stretch and soar,
We'll seek the wonders, forevermore.
For beyond the shore, the soul ignites,
In the dance of waves, we find our lights.

Whispers of the Untamed

In shadows deep where wild things roam,
The whispers of the forest call home.
Rustling leaves and secrets shared,
Nature's breath, gentle and bared.

Moonlight glimmers on the stream,
Painting night with a silver dream.
Creatures stir in the quiet dark,
Each one bearing its own spark.

Starlit skies hold tales untold,
Of spirits fierce and hearts so bold.
A symphony of life at play,
In whispers soft, they find their way.

With every rustle, a story unfolds,
Of hidden paths and life it molds.
The untamed breathes, so wild and free,
In whispers shared, it speaks to me.

Echoes Among the Tall Pines

Beneath the boughs where shadows dwell,
Echoes of the forest's spell.
Pines stand tall, guardians strong,
Whispering the age-old song.

Wind carries tales of days long past,
Of time that sways, yet holds steadfast.
Every rustle sings of grace,
Nature inviting us to embrace.

Birds call out from their lofty perches,
Their melodies, a quiet search.
Among the pines, the heart finds peace,
In echoes sweet, all troubles cease.

With every breeze, memories swirl,
Among the pines, life's colors unfurl.
A sacred space where spirits roam,
In echoes deep, we find our home.

Breath of the Open Plains

Across the fields where wildflowers sway,
The breath of the plains whispers play.
Golden grasses dance and bow,
In the sunlight's warm embrace now.

Skies stretch wide, a canvas so clear,
Filled with dreams that draw us near.
Windswept whispers carry far,
Guiding hearts like a wandering star.

The horizon calls with an open hand,
Inviting souls to take a stand.
Freedom sings in every breeze,
Among the plains, we find our ease.

Every step on this endless ground,
In the breath of nature, peace is found.
A journey deep where spirits soar,
In the open plains, we seek for more.

Dance of the Rugged Peaks

In rugged heights where eagles soar,
The dance of mountains forever more.
Stone and sky entwined with grace,
Carving echoes in this sacred space.

Glaciers whisper tales of old,
Of nature's strength, a sight so bold.
Clouds embrace the towering crest,
In this wild place, our hearts find rest.

The sun dips low, painting the stone,
A dance of colors, bright and alone.
Each peak embraces the fading light,
Holding secrets of day and night.

In the shadows, whispers abide,
Of ancient tales and the mystic tide.
Among the rugged, dreams take flight,
In peaks that dance, hearts ignite.

The Gaze of the Watchful Stars

In the stillness of night, they glow,
Silent watchers from far below.
Whispers of stories, untold dreams,
Guiding the lost with silver beams.

Each flicker a promise, each twinkle a sigh,
Tales of the ages that drift through the sky.
A canvas of wonder, so vast and so deep,
Cradling secrets that the universe keeps.

They dance in the silence, a celestial show,
Painting our hearts with a luminous flow.
In their watchful gaze, we find our way,
As night fades gently into the day.

From Thorns to Blossoms

In the garden where shadows loom,
A seedling grows, dispelling gloom.
Thorns may prick, but roots hold tight,
Emerging beauty, a bold delight.

Petals unfold in the warm sun's grace,
Colors erupting, each in its place.
A symphony painted in vibrant hues,
Whispers of nature, a soft muse.

Through trials that twist and moments that sting,
Life finds a way to bloom and sing.
With every struggle, each heart will find,
From thorns to blossoms, true love is blind.

Chasing Shadows at Dusk

As daylight fades, shadows creep,
Whispering secrets that silence keep.
Fingers of twilight stretch and sway,
Guiding the dreamers who linger and play.

The horizon blurs in a twilight dance,
Inviting the wanderers, lost in a trance.
With every breath, the night draws near,
Chasing the echoes, embracing the fear.

Stars will emerge in the velvet sky,
Catching the glimmers of shadows that fly.
In the chase of the night, we find our way,
In the dance with the darkness, we learn to stay.

Colors of the Hidden Valleys

In valleys kissed by the softest light,
Nature reveals its radiant sight.
Colors unfurl in a gentle embrace,
A symphony woven with delicate grace.

Emerald greens and sapphire streams,
Mingles with echoes of sunlit dreams.
Petals of gold and hues of the dawn,
Paint tales of wonder, never withdrawn.

Each turn of the path, a fresh new surprise,
Nature's own palette before our eyes.
In hidden corners where whispers reside,
Colors of valleys, our souls open wide.

Echoes of the Ancient Winds

Whispers dance on gentle breeze,
Carrying tales from yesteryear.
Through the valleys, through the trees,
Ancient voices loud and clear.

Tales of battles, love, and strife,
Woven in the fabric of time.
Each gust breathes a story to life,
Chants of ages, soft yet prime.

Moonlight filters, shadows play,
In the silence, secrets stir.
Night unveils what dreams relay,
Echoes found in nature's purr.

Rise and fall of twilight's song,
Harmony of earth and sky.
In the whispering winds so strong,
We find the past, we learn to fly.

Harmonies of the Wandering Soul

In the heart where shadows blend,
A melody begins to rise.
Echoes of a journey's end,
Dancing amidst the starry skies.

Each step forward, notes unfold,
A symphony of paths untread.
Stories waiting to be told,
In the music where dreams are fed.

Flowing rivers, mountains high,
Nature's chorus, wild and free.
Fleeting moments drift and fly,
Crafting harmonies for me.

Whispers call from dawn's embrace,
Guiding me through night and day.
In the wandering, I find grace,
In every note, I break away.

The Sigh of the Distant Mountains

Veiled in mist, their secrets hold,
Whispers of the earth's deep breath.
Ancient giants, proud and bold,
Crowned in snow, untouched by death.

Echoing their silent plea,
Stirring winds through rocky caves.
In their presence, wild and free,
Nature speaks, the spirit braves.

Underneath the starry glow,
Mountain sighs a tranquil tune.
In their shadows, dreams may grow,
Kissed by light of silver moon.

Journey calls, a path unknown,
Up to heights where eagles soar.
In their whispers, seeds are sown,
The adventure lies in store.

In the Heart of the Untamed

Where the wild rivers meander swift,
And the forest breathes a sigh.
Nature's canvas, a precious gift,
In the heart, wild spirits lie.

Branches weave tales in the air,
Each leaf a story yet to share.
Adventures beckon everywhere,
Calling souls to venture there.

Sunlight dances on the ground,
Mapping paths of dreams once dreamed.
In the silence, peace is found,
In the wild, imagination streamed.

Time stands still, the world unfurls,
In the embrace of earth's own hand.
Lost within, the heart twirls,
In the heart of the untamed land.

Journey to the Heart of Nature

In the whispering trees, secrets unfold,
Nature's embrace, a story retold.
Birds sing softly, a melody clear,
Guiding the wanderer, drawing them near.

Streams flow gently, sparkling with light,
Crickets sing lullabies, calming the night.
Mountains stand tall, with wisdom that's deep,
In this tranquil realm, my soul finds its keep.

Flowers burst forth, a vibrant delight,
Colors entwined, painting the sight.
Sunrise spills gold on the waking earth,
Each moment a treasure, a testament of worth.

Beneath the vast sky, I drift and I dream,
Nature's pure heartbeat, a soft-flowing stream.
In her wild arms, I find my true place,
Journeying onward, in nature's embrace.

The Unraveled Pathways

Among the shadows, the paths intertwine,
Footsteps echo softly, a call divine.
Each fork in the road holds stories untold,
Whispers of past travelers, brave and bold.

Leaves crunch beneath me, a symphony bright,
Guiding my spirit beneath the pale light.
Roots stretch beneath, weaving tales of old,
Treading the pathways, both timid and bold.

A fork leads to laughter, the other to tears,
Each choice a reflection of hopes and fears.
The journey's the canvas where we paint our way,
The pathway unravels as night turns to day.

In the dance of the twilight, the compass will sway,
Leading us forward, come what may.
With each turn I take, I embrace the unknown,
For the unraveling journey is where I have grown.

Serenade of the Highland Mist

In the early dawn, where the mist does play,
Highland whispers beckon the light of the day.
Echoes of histories linger in air,
Nature's soft serenade, precious and rare.

Heath blooms wild, in purple and gold,
Caught in the beauty, the mysteries told.
A symphony of silence, a call to the heart,
In the cradle of mountains, the magic will start.

The lochs mirror skies, a tranquil embrace,
Reflections of dreams in a serene space.
Grassy knolls rise, as the sun kisses down,
Woven with threads of the ancient and brown.

As shadows retreat and the day takes its throne,
The Highland mist sings, a soft, haunting tone.
In each breath, a promise, in each step, a guide,
In the serenade of mist, forever I bide.

Lament of the Distant Stars

In the velvet night, where silence reigns,
Stars whisper stories through luminous veins.
Each flicker a memory from ages past,
Glimmers of hope that forever will last.

They sigh for lost worlds, forgotten and rare,
Cloaked in the shadows of cosmic despair.
Yet in their lament, a beauty unfolds,
A dance of the heavens, both gentle and bold.

Constellations murmur, a soothing refrain,
Charting the courses of joy and of pain.
With every twinkle, a tear set free,
In the vastness of space, a shared destiny.

Though distant they are, their light reaches near,
Guiding the dreamer with warmth and with cheer.
In the lament of stars, a promise we hear,
That the vastness of night holds the light we revere.

Currents of the Forgotten Trails

Whispers of the ancient ways,
They call the hearts that roam.
In shadows, secrets softly play,
Among the trees, far from home.

The river hums a lullaby,
As stones speak stories old.
Each ripple tells a silent sigh,
Of dreams that once were bold.

Footsteps fade, the world moves on,
Yet echoes linger still.
In twilight's glow, the paths are drawn,
With silent, timeless will.

To wander here is to embrace,
The tales of those long gone.
In every bend, a hint of grace,
Where memories live on.

Footfalls on Untrodden Paths

In the thicket where shadows lie,
New journeys whisper low.
With every step beneath the sky,
A world begins to grow.

Grass bends softly to the quest,
Adventures yet unseen.
With every heartbeat, life's a test,
In spaces tucked between.

Nature holds a breathless pause,
A canvas fresh and bright.
Each footfall writes a silent cause,
In realms of pure delight.

Destiny in every glance,
Where paths gently unfurl.
In stillness lies a secret dance,
The pulse of this vast world.

Serenade of the Open Skies

Above the fields where silence reigns,
The lull of clouds drifts slow.
In sunlight's warmth, the spirit gains,
As breezes softly blow.

Stars awaken in the night,
With dreams that never fade.
The moon becomes a guiding light,
In twilight's serenade.

Whispers of the wind do weave,
A melody so clear.
In nature's arms, I dare believe,
That hope is ever near.

To dance beneath the vast expanse,
And feel the world embrace,
Each fleeting moment is a chance,
To savor boundless grace.

Breezes over Barren Mountains

The peaks stand tall, a silent choir,
With stories etched in stone.
Beneath the sky, a wild desire,
For realms that feel like home.

Dusty trails where few have trod,
Whisper tales of might.
In every crevice, life at odds,
With stars that shine so bright.

Breezes weave through rocky seams,
A melody of peace.
In solitude, I chase my dreams,
Where heartache finds release.

Among the rugged, raw terrain,
Resilience sings its song.
In barren lands, where hope remains,
The spirit carries on.

Secrets in the Swirling Breeze

Whispers dance through the tall grass,
A melody soft as the twilight hour.
Forgotten tales of the past endure,
Carried by winds with gentle power.

Leaves murmur secrets, drift and sway,
Casting shadows on the forest floor.
The swirling breeze, a gentle guide,
Holds ancient stories forevermore.

In silent corners where shadows cling,
Nature speaks in a hushed refrain.
With each gust that brushes my skin,
I feel the heartbeat of the earth's domain.

Under the stars, beneath the trees,
I listen close to the night's embrace.
For in the whispers, and the breeze,
I find a truth, a sacred space.

Flight of the Feathered Wanderers

High above, they spread their wings,
With grace that dances in the sky.
Feathered hearts in endless search,
Chasing dreams as moments fly.

Through azure heights and golden rays,
They carve their paths with joyful cries.
Unity found in every flick,
Wanderers beneath the vast, wide skies.

Across the mountains, and through the trees,
They soar with purpose, wild and free.
Each flight a tale of where they've been,
A journey whispered on the breeze.

As dusk descends and shadows fall,
They gather close to rest and dream.
In the quiet hush, their stories blend,
In the night's embrace, their spirits gleam.

Roar of the Untouched Valleys

In the distance, a thunderous sound,
Echoes through the ancient stone.
The valleys roar, wild and proud,
A symphony of nature's own.

Unraveling secrets of untamed lands,
Where rivers carve their tales anew.
Majestic peaks kiss the sky,
Guardians of the valley's view.

Through the wild grasses and fragrant blooms,
The spirit of earth begins to rise.
Each echo tells of time and place,
Whispers woven in the skies.

Here lies the heart, untouched and pure,
In silence, the valleys breathe and sigh.
A legacy of strength and grace,
Roaring softly under the sky.

Symphony of the Roaming Hills

The hills awaken with dawn's soft light,
A canvas brushed with golden hues.
Nature's symphony begins to play,
As morning's chorus breaks the blues.

Rustling leaves and chirping birds,
Compose a melody so sweet.
Each note a dance of life and love,
As rhythms guide my wandering feet.

The trails wind through emerald grass,
Whispers echo from vale to crest.
With every step, a story weaves,
In the arms of hills, my heart finds rest.

As twilight drapes her velvet cloak,
The hills breathe deep, their secrets known.
In the twilight's glow, my spirit sings,
In this symphony, I am never alone.

Pulses of the Untamed Wilderness

Deep in the thicket, shadows play,
The wild whispers secrets of the day.
Roots intertwine in a dancer's embrace,
Nature's heart thumps in a timeless space.

Crisp air carries scents both sweet and wild,
In every rustle, the earth's own child.
A deer leaps softly, its grace unmatched,
While crickets keep rhythm, nature's own patched.

Stars pierce the night with shimmering light,
Owls call from trees, their wisdom in flight.
Under the moon, the world softly sighs,
The spirit of wildness never truly dies.

All around, life pulses, wild and free,
In the wilderness, it's just you and me.
Each heartbeat echoes, a boundless roar,
In the dance of the wild, we long for more.

Footprints on Forgotten Trails

Moss-covered pathways, where few dare to tread,
Each step whispers stories of those long dead.
Sunlight dapples through leaves overhead,
Nature holds secrets, where dreams have fled.

With every turn, a memory awakes,
Rustling leaves mark the history it makes.
The whisper of hikers, long lost in time,
Echoes through valleys in rhythmic rhyme.

Wildflowers bloom where the heart once wandered,
In the silence of twilight, we pondered.
Footprints may fade, but the path stays bold,
In every shadow, a story retold.

So let us walk softly, with hearts open wide,
Embracing the past as our faithful guide.
For the trails we traverse linger far and near,
Footprints of memories, forever dear.

Harmony of the Enchanted Glades

In glades of emerald, sunlight spills,
Where magic stirs and nature fills.
The hum of life in a gentle stream,
Every moment here feels like a dream.

Whispers of breezes weave through the trees,
Tickle the petals of flowers at ease.
Ferns sway gracefully, lost in the song,
In this vibrant realm, we all belong.

Birds serenade from canopies high,
Notes intertwine with the softest sigh.
Mushrooms bloom, painting the ground with delight,
In enchanted glades, our spirits take flight.

Together we dance, with earth as our stage,
Lost in the beauty, we forget every cage.
Harmony calls from the wild, pure and grand,
In the embrace of nature, together we stand.

The Melody of Nature's Breath

Hear the soft whisper of the rustling leaves,
A melody woven through nature's eaves.
The brook's lilting laughter, a soothing refrain,
Dancing on stones, like a sweet, gentle rain.

Mountains hum softly in their timeless grace,
Where winds carry tunes across every space.
The sigh of the valleys, lush and profound,
In the deep silence, true beauty is found.

With each breath of nature, a rhythm takes flight,
Life pulses as one in the warm, golden light.
The heartbeat of earth can be felt in the still,
A symphony born from the vastness and thrill.

So close your eyes, let the music flow,
Feel every note, let your spirit grow.
In the harmony found in the wild's gentle breath,
Lies a promise of beauty, beyond life and death.

Songs from the Hidden Meadows

In meadows green, where silence sings,
The whispering winds, like gentle strings,
Dance with the breeze, a soft ballet,
As nature hums its tune each day.

With petals bright, their colors play,
In golden light, they sway and sway,
The joyful chirps of birds take flight,
Compose a symphony of pure delight.

Beneath the shade of ancient trees,
A calmness drifts upon the breeze,
While shadows stretch and whispers fade,
In hidden meadows, peace is laid.

So let us pause, and for a while,
Embrace the beauty, share a smile,
For in these songs, our hearts take wing,
In hidden meadows, life does sing.

Drifting Dust and Dappled Light

In golden rays that filter through,
The dancing dust, like dreams come true,
A soft embrace, the day's embrace,
In dappled light, we find our place.

Each moment glows, with magic spun,
In pathways bright, we chase the sun,
With every step, new journeys birth,
In drifting dust, we wander earth.

Through shadowed glades, where secrets hide,
The whispers call, our hearts collide,
In flickering light, we find our way,
Drifting dust at end of day.

So let us pause, and breathe it in,
The world alive, where dreams begin,
In dappled light, we dance and sway,
In drifting dust, we'll find our way.

Glimpse of the Endless Horizon

Beyond the hills, where heavens meet,
An endless line, a path so sweet,
With every step, a heart takes flight,
Towards a dream in morning light.

A world awaits, so vast and new,
In shades of gold and skies of blue,
To seek, to find, to ever roam,
In endless horizons, we find home.

With every wave that kisses sand,
The ocean sings, a grand command,
To chase the sun, to seek the stars,
In endless horizons, love is ours.

So let us wander, hearts ablaze,
Through fields of hope, in twilight's haze,
For in each glimpse, our spirits soar,
Endless horizons, forevermore.

Canvas of the Changing Seasons

A canvas stretched, where colors blend,
In hues of red, as autumn sends,
With every leaf, a story told,
In nature's art, the world unfolds.

In winter's grasp, a blanket white,
The quiet calm, a peaceful night,
With frosty breath, the world grows still,
In frozen dreams, we feel the thrill.

As springtime blooms, the flowers rise,
In fragrant scents, beneath the skies,
A symphony of life's rebirth,
In changing seasons, we find worth.

In summer's glow, the sun does shine,
With laughter free, our hearts align,
A canvas true, of life's design,
In changing seasons, love entwined.

Roaming Hearts in the Wild

In the forest deep and wide,
Hearts roam free, side by side.
Whispers carried by the breeze,
Nature's song brings us to ease.

Through the thickets, shadows play,
Sunlight guides us on our way.
With every step, the joy unfolds,
Adventure waits, our hearts are bold.

Beneath the stars, we share a dream,
Together, lost in nature's theme.
Bound by ties, our spirits soar,
Roaming hearts seek evermore.

In wild meadows, time stands still,
Nature's magic, purest thrill.
With every heartbeat, worlds align,
Together, roaming, hearts entwined.

Flickers of Flame and Feather

In twilight's glow, the embers dance,
A flicker sparks, invokes romance.
Feathers rise on whispers light,
Binding dreams in the night.

With every flicker, stories weave,
Tales of love that we believe.
Ashes fall, like gentle rain,
Yet from the fire, we rise again.

Softly glowing, the night unfolds,
Secrets held like treasures bold.
Feathered hearts, entwined in grace,
Flickers of flame, a warm embrace.

When dawn breaks, shadows fall,
Memories linger, we recall.
In the quiet of a brand new day,
Flickers fade, but love will stay.

The Dance of Earth and Sky

In the morning's golden light,
Earth and sky take their flight.
Mountains rise and rivers flow,
Nature's rhythm, a perfect show.

Clouds drift softly, a gentle sway,
Stars still whisper of yesterday.
In twilight's hush, colors blend,
The dance continues, without end.

Roots dig deep, reaching wide,
While whispers of the winds abide.
Skyward dreams on the horizon,
In this dance, our hearts will rise on.

Hand in hand, we celebrate,
The harmony that speaks of fate.
In every turn, our spirits fly,
Together, we dance, earth and sky.

Nature's Gentle Caress

In the morning's soft embrace,
Nature whispers, leaves trace.
Butterflies twirl, colors bright,
In the warmth of sacred light.

Kisses of wind, a tender breeze,
Brings the scent of blooming trees.
Each moment filled with heartfelt grace,
In nature's arms, we find our place.

Gentle rivers sing their song,
In their flow, we all belong.
With every wave, a sweet caress,
Nature breathes, we find our rest.

At twilight's edge, the stars ignite,
Nature's lullaby, pure delight.
In her cradle, dreams take flight,
Wrapped in peace, all feels right.

The Melody of Hidden Trails

In shadows deep, where whispers play,
Footsteps trace the paths of gray.
Leaves like secrets, softly sigh,
As dreams in silence drift and fly.

Beneath the boughs, the twilight hums,
A tune of nature, soft becomes.
The heartbeats dance, the echoes call,
Together swaying, one and all.

Through tangled woods, the light will wane,
Yet through the dark, new visions gain.
Each winding turn, a tale retold,
Of the brave and the bold.

With every step, the world unfolds,
In hidden trails where magic holds.
A melody sung, a journey bright,
Awakening dreams within the night.

Whirlwinds of the Lost Echoes

Caught in the dance of swirling air,
Fleeting whispers, light as a prayer.
Voices of past, they softly sweep,
In the whirlwind, secrets deep.

Lost in time, the echoes twirl,
Remnants of thoughts begin to unfurl.
Each whisper a story, longing to stay,
In the melancholy of yesterday.

Through barren lands, the shadows race,
Chasing the dreams that time won't lace.
A tempest brews, the heart will strain,
As memories flutter, wild and vain.

Whirling fast, they lose their form,
In the chaos, find the norm.
Caught in the midst of love and pain,
The lost echoes call again.

Tides of Forgotten Memories

The ocean breathes with ancient sighs,
Waves crashing softly, whispering lies.
Carried ashore, the dreams of old,
In tides of memories, stories unfold.

Seashells hold moments, lost in the sea,
Grains of sand, where hearts used to be.
A lullaby sung by the moon's pale light,
Guiding the lost through the velvet night.

With every tide that pulls away,
A piece of the past in the light of day.
Seagulls call to the winds of change,
While memories linger, sweet yet strange.

Awash with the rhythm of ebb and flow,
What once was molten is now aglow.
The tides will rise, and thus they fall,
In forgotten dreams, we recall.

The Creep of Twilight's Adventure

As daylight fades, the shadows creep,
Inviting tales from slumbering sleep.
In twilight's grasp, the world transforms,
Where magic lingers and wonder warms.

Each whispered breeze reveals a gate,
To realms unknown, where dreams await.
With every step, the stars ignite,
Painting the canvas of the night.

Through forest paths and starlit streams,
The heart awakens to woven dreams.
An adventure born in shades of dusk,
To wander free, to seek, to trust.

In twilight's whisper, the spirits dance,
Unraveling tales of fleeting chance.
Embrace the night, let the journey start,
For in the twilight, lies the heart.

Nature's Echo in the Stillness

In the shade of ancient trees,
Whispers float on gentle breeze.
Leaves like whispers softly sigh,
Nature's echo, sweetly nigh.

Rivers murmur, secrets shared,
Every moment, heart ensnared.
Mountains stand, a stoic grace,
Time becomes a tender space.

Flowers bloom in vibrant hues,
Painting earth with morning's dew.
Birds take flight in crystal air,
Nature's song, beyond compare.

In this realm of peace and light,
Stillness wraps the heart so tight.
Nature's echo, calm and true,
Lingers soft in me and you.

Journey through the Misty Outlands

Through the fog, the shadows creep,
Secrets that the wild keep.
Footsteps quiet on the trail,
Adventure calls through misted veil.

Whispers of the ancient lore,
Hidden paths to worlds explore.
Every turn a mystery,
In the fog, we're wild and free.

Echoes dance in twilight's grace,
Nature's call, an embrace.
With each breath, the journey flows,
Through the mist, the spirit grows.

Voices linger in the night,
Guiding hearts with gentle light.
In this realm of dreams unfurled,
Traveling through a mystic world.

Seasons of the Lost Winds

Autumn leaves like whispered dreams,
Drifting down in hazy streams.
Winter's breath, a silent chill,
Time stands still upon the hill.

Spring awakens, colors rise,
Life springs forth beneath blue skies.
Summer's warmth, a fiery glow,
Each season paints a tale to show.

Lost winds carry stories old,
In their rush, the past is told.
Each moment, fleeting, swift,
A treasure found, a precious gift.

Cycles turn, like tides at sea,
Seasons dance in harmony.
In the flow, we find our place,
Breath of time, a sweet embrace.

The Breath of the Untamed Essence

Whispers of the wild untamed,
In every heartbeat, life is named.
Rivers carve through ancient stone,
Nature's breath, a sacred tone.

Mountains rise to kiss the sky,
Where dreams and earthbound hopes comply.
Forests whisper tales of old,
In their shadows, strength unfolds.

Stars ignite the velvet night,
Guiding souls with radiant light.
In the depth of nature's song,
We find heartbeats where we belong.

Feel the wild, embrace the call,
In the dance, we find it all.
The breath of essence, fierce and free,
Bound by nature's harmony.

Threads of Adventure in the Unknown

Beneath the stars, a path unfolds,
A journey waits, its story told.
With every step, the shadows dance,
In magic's grip, we take a chance.

Through tangled woods and rivers wide,
With courage deep, we'll turn the tide.
The whispers call, the night is young,
In every heartbeat, dreams are sung.

New lands will greet us, bright and bold,
A tapestry of tales untold.
Adventure's thread, we proudly weave,
In the unknown, we dare believe.

With every twist, we find our way,
In light and dark, we choose to stay.
The world awaits with open arms,
To guide our souls through lovely charms.

The Heartbeat of the Forgotten Lands

In distant realms where shadows play,
The heartbeats echo, night and day.
Forgotten tales in ancient tongue,
By nature's grace, our songs are sung.

Beneath the trees, a whisper calls,
A memory that gently falls.
With every stone, a story lies,
Of lands once lost to time's own sighs.

The rivers murmur secrets old,
In every ripple, life unfolds.
With every breeze, the past returns,
A flame of hope forever burns.

In these sacred spaces, we roam,
Through roots of earth, we find our home.
United with the pulse of sand,
We cherish life in the forgotten land.

Whispers Through the Thicket

In the thicket, shadows move,
A serenade of nature's groove.
With rustling leaves, the stories share,
The secrets linger in the air.

Through tangled vines and petals bright,
The whispers carry day and night.
Each soft rustle, a tale revealed,
In the heart's embrace, the truth is healed.

Beneath the boughs, we pause and hear,
The ancient songs that draw us near.
With every breath, the earth does sigh,
The thicket speaks, as time goes by.

In hidden paths where spirits dwell,
The beauty of nature casts its spell.
We wander through this sacred space,
In whispers soft, we find our place.

Echoes of Distant Peaks

The mountains rise, a timeless throne,
In distant peaks, where echoes moan.
With each ascent, the spirits call,
Their wisdom shared with those who fall.

Through rugged trails and clouds of white,
We seek the stars, a guiding light.
The sun dips low, a fiery hue,
On peaks of gold, the evening's due.

Each echo carries tales of old,
Of warriors brave and hearts of gold.
With every step, the echoes grow,
In silent realms, new dreams we sow.

As night unfolds, the world stands still,
In the mountain's heart, we find our will.
With every breath, we feel the climb,
In distant peaks, we conquer time.